GIRAFFES

By Melissa Cole
Photographs by Tom and Pat Leeson

BLACKBIRCH®
PRESS

THOMSON
★
GALE

San Diego • Detroit • New York • San Francisco • Cleveland • New Haven, Conn. • Waterville, Maine • London • Munich

THOMSON

GALE

For more information, contact
The Gale Group, Inc.
27500 Drake Rd.
Farmington Hills, MI 48331-3535
Or you can visit our Internet site at http://www.gale.com

Photo Credits: Cover, all photos © Tom and Pat Leeson Nature Wildlife Photography; back cover © CORBIS; pages 7, 19, 20 © McDonald Wildlife Photography

LIBRARY OF CONGRESS CATALOGING-IN-PUBLICATION DATA

Cole, Melissa S.
  Giraffes / by Melissa S. Cole.
    v. cm. — (wild Africa series)
  Contents: The body of a giraffe — Social life — The mating game — Giraffes and humans.
  ISBN 1-56711-634-5 (hardback : alk. paper)
  1. Giraffe—Juvenile literature. [1. Giraffe.] I. Title.
  QL737.U56 C66 2003
  599.638—dc21   2002003379

Printed in China
10 9 8 7 6 5 4 3 2 1

Contents

Introduction

What creature is taller than any other animal on earth? A giraffe! In fact, the word "giraffe" comes from the Arabic word *zarafah*, which means "the tallest of animals," or "one that walks very fast."

Giraffes are related to antelopes and deer. Giraffe bones have been found in Spain, Hungary, Greece, Iran, India, Pakistan, and Africa. Climate changes caused the world to become colder.

Left: Giraffes are the tallest animals on earth.
Right: Giraffes live in central and South Africa.

4

This caused many giraffe species to become extinct. Although only one species of giraffe (Giraffa camelopardalis) survives today, scientists recognize nine different subspecies, or races. Today, these amazing animals live in a narrow strip across the center of Africa. They also live in a small section of South Africa.

The Giraffe's Body

Giraffes are the tallest of all land animals. Male giraffes, called bulls, are usually larger than female giraffes, called cows. Adult males can weigh up to 3,000 pounds (1,360.8 kg). They usually stand between 15 and 17 (4.6–5.2 m) feet tall. The biggest bull ever measured was 19 feet high (5.8 m)! Female giraffes usually stand about 14 feet tall (4.3 m). They can weigh as much as 2,500 pounds (1,134 kg).

Giraffes have thick skin. It protects them from the weather. It also keeps them from being hurt by the thorns on the trees they eat. Giraffe hair is short and smooth like that of a horse.

Male giraffes can be up to 17 feet (5 m) tall!

Different types of giraffes have slightly different spot patterns on their hair. Masai and Nubian giraffes have dark, uneven spots that blend in with their hair. Reticulated giraffes have smooth, even patches. This makes them look as though a cream-colored net has been thrown over their brown bodies.

Scientists think that the spots and patches on a giraffe's skin help it to blend in with its surroundings. When a giraffe stands in a fores, its long neck may look like just another tree trunk.

A giraffe's heart is 2 feet (.6 m) long and weighs 25 pounds (11.3 kg). It is big enough to pump blood to the lungs, brain, and hooves. Arteries (tubes that carry blood from the heart to the rest of the body) in their necks helps keep

Spots help giraffes to blend in with their surroundings.

Giraffes' legs are almost twice as long as their bodies.

giraffes' blood from rushing to their brain when they lower their heads to eat or drink. If blood moves to their brains too quickly, giraffes might get dizzy or fall down.

Giraffes walk differently than most animals. This is because their legs are almost twice as long as their bodies. To keep from tripping over their feet, giraffes move both legs on the same side of their bodies at the same time. Their necks and heads move back and forth. This helps giraffes keep their balance. Giraffes can gallop at speeds of more than 30 miles (48 km) per hour. They run in a similar way to jackrabbits. Their back legs spread apart. Their forelegs are tucked close together between their back legs. This allows them to run very fast.

Giraffes never go into water to bathe, because they cannot swim. To get clean, they scratch and lick themselves or each other. Giraffes rub their necks and rumps against rough tree trunks. They can even clean their nostrils with their own tongues! Birds called oxpeckers, or tickbirds, often ride on giraffe's necks and backs. These birds eat annoying insects. They also remove loose hair, dirt, and dry skin.

Special Features

All giraffes have at least two horns. Reticulated and Masai bulls have a third, bump-like horn between their eyes. Rothschild's giraffes have two small extra horns. They sit toward the front of the head. Giraffe horns are not like those found on antelope and cattle. A young giraffe's horns are made of a soft, flexible substance called cartilage. Cartilage is gradually replaced by bone as the horns grow larger. Bull giraffes horns are about 9 inches (22.9 cm) long. They are much thicker than a female's horns. Horns continue to grow throughout a giraffe's life.

Giraffes have sharp eyesight. They can spot danger more quickly than many other animals. Their large eyes are widely spaced on either side of their heads.

Giraffes have at least two horns on their heads.

This gives them a wide field of vision. Their long necks allow giraffes to see things far off in the distance. Zebras, ostriches, antelope, wildebeests, and other animals stay close to giraffes to stay safe. Giraffes twitch their tails when they spot danger. When other animals see this sign, they know to gallop away.

Big eyes mean giraffes have excellent eyesight.

Social Life

Giraffes are peaceful, social animals. They often form small family groups of 3 to 15 giraffes. These groups consist mainly of females and their young, called calves. Young males stay with the family group until they are teenagers. At this time, they are chased away by the females. When this happens, young bulls often join an all-male group. All-male groups are called bachelor groups.

Giraffes form family groups of 3 to 15 members.

An older, dominant male leads each bachelor group. Bulls fight to decide who will lead a bachelor group. They move their heads and necks in a certain way. This is called neck knocking. The 2 challengers move away from the group. They stand side by side. They spread out their front legs for balance. One giraffe lowers his head. He swings it against the other's neck. This giraffe tries to move away and swing his head toward his challenger. A bull giraffe's head may weigh more than 25 pounds (11.3 kg), so these blows can really hurt!

After about 15 minutes of fighting, the weaker giraffe retreats. Once the 2 giraffes have decided which is the dominant animal, they rejoin the herd. They will feed side by side—they even rub their necks together!

Giraffes rub their necks together in a kind of hug.

Giraffes communicate mainly through gestures. They are able to make noises such as low moans or snorts, but they are usually silent. Mothers call their calves with a low whistle.

Giraffes do not form strong bonds with each other. They often separate from one group and join another one. Small groups may join together to feed. Groups separate if there is not enough food in one area.

Two or three hundred giraffes may live in a feeding area, or home range. This area can be more than 1,500 square miles (2,414 km). Giraffes stay within their home range as long as there is enough to eat. Giraffes may migrate (move) to areas where there is more food during the dry season.

Giraffes migrate (move) during the dry season to where there is enough food.

Feeding

Giraffes are herbivores, or plant eaters. They eat about 75 pounds (34 kg) of vegetation each day. Giraffes browse on shoots and leaves of many plants and trees. They also eat twigs, seedpods, and fruit.

Their favorite food is the leaves of the spiny acacia tree. Most animals avoid acacia trees because of their three-inch long thorns. But the thorns do not bother giraffes. A giraffe's upper lip is covered with tough skin and long hairs. This protects it against thorns and stinging ants that live on acacia leaves. A thick, moist coating protects a giraffe's tongue.

Giraffes hve tough skin on their upper lips. This protects them from thorns when they eat.

To feed, a giraffe sticks its long black tongue out more than 18 inches (45.7 cm) to get between the thorns. A giraffe wraps its long tongue around a bunch of young leaves. It brings them to its mouth. A giraffe does not have front teeth, so it clips off twigs and leaves by pressing its bottom teeth against the roof of its mouth. Then it grinds up the leaves with flat molar teeth in the back of its mouth. Acacias contain almost all of the nutrients a giraffe needs except salt and calcium. To get these minerals, giraffes lick natural salt deposits. They also chew on the bones of dead animals.

A giraffe's stomach is divided into four sections. Food goes into the first compartment, where it is mixed with saliva and stomach juices. Water passes directly into the second stomach.

A giraffe uses its tongue to bring leaves into its mouth.

While giraffes rest, food is formed into lumps called cuds. Cuds are brought back up into a giraffe's mouth to be chewed more thoroughly. It chews each cud for about a minute, swallows it, and then brings up another. The cuds then go into the third and fourth stomachs to be completely digested.

Acacia leaves contain almost 75 percent water, so giraffes do not need to drink very often. If water is plentiful, giraffes drink about once every two or three days. They only drink when they feel completely safe. Their necks are not long enough to reach the water when they stand. To drink, they have to bend their front legs or spread them wide apart. This puts them in a difficult position. And they are more vulnerable to predators. When giraffes visit water holes, they often take turns drinking. A few giraffes keep watch while the others drink. A giraffe can drink up to ten gallons of water at one time.

A giraffe spreads its front legs apart so it can reach down low to drink.

The Mating Game

A dominant bull joins a family group of giraffes when he is ready to mate. Females can mate when they are 4 or 5 years old. They can have babies until they are about 20 years old. Females are ready to mate once every 2 weeks. During this time, their urine has chemicals in it that attract bull giraffes.

A bull follows a cow around to let her know he wants to mate. He grazes beside her. And he rubs his neck and head against hers. After mating, the bull and the cow return to feeding. Eventually, the male leaves the group. The cow will raise the calf without his help.

A bull follows a cow to let her know he wants to mate.

Raising Young

A female giraffe is pregnant for about 15 months. Most giraffe mothers give birth alone. They find a hidden spot without tall grass and bushes where predators might hide.

A giraffe gives birth standing up. She bends her legs slightly to shorten the baby's fall. A calf is born headfirst. It drops about 5 feet (1.5 m) to the ground. The mother licks the baby clean. This removes odors that might attract predators. It also increases the baby's blood circulation.

The newborn is 6 feet (1.8 m) tall and weighs 120 to 150 pounds (54.4–68 kg). Its horns are small cartilage bumps with spiky bristles of hair on them. A calf usually stands on its own within 10 minutes of birth. It begins to nurse an hour later.

A cow licks her calf clean to remove birth smells.

Giraffe cows hide their calves in tall grass or under bushes while they graze. They return often to let the baby nurse. Calves cannot outrun predators. If a calf is attacked when its mother is nearby, it will run to her and hide beneath her belly. Mother giraffes fiercely protect their calves. Still, lions and hyenas kill half of all giraffe babies within their first week of life.

Calves feed on plants when they are 2 weeks old. They continue to nurse, though, because their necks are too short to drink water. When a calf is one month old, it and its mother join a family group. Each morning, mothers take their calves to a special clearing, or nursery area.

A calf nurses until its neck is long enough to drink water.

Calves lie down or nibble acacia bushes. Sometimes they play games, chase each other, and jump around. Female giraffes take turns caring for the calves.

Mothers return from feeding several times a day to nurse their young. In the evening, the whole group returns to protect the calves overnight.

Calves grow quickly their first year. They may gain an inch (2.5 cm) or more of height each day. Four-month-old calves can run fast enough to escape predators. But they often stay with their mothers for one to two years.

Mother giraffes lick, nuzzle, and rub necks with their calves. They use their teeth to clean their young. After 2 years, cows no longer care for their calves. Female calves often stay in the same group as their mothers. Males are chased away to join a bachelor group.

A mother giraffe is affectionate with her calf.

21

Giraffes and Humans

African people have hunted giraffes for hundreds of years. Hunting giraffes for food and sport has caused a decline in their population. Giraffes nearly disappeared at the beginning of the 20th century. This is when giraffe hunting became popular with Europeans. To protect the decreasing giraffe population, parks and reserves were created.

These protected areas are important to maintain the giraffe population. As Africa's human population grows, farms and villages use up much of the giraffe's habitat. In western Africa, giraffes are increasingly rare. They have completely disappeared from certain regions.

Parks and reserves were created to protect giraffe habitats.

Giraffes are protected in all African countries. African governments and animal rights groups work to prevent people from hunting giraffes. Still, illegal hunting continues for giraffe skins and tails. The bristles of a giraffe's tail are used to make heavy-duty thread, good-luck bracelets, and flyswatters. Giraffe skin is used to make blankets and rugs.

No one knows exactly how many giraffes remain. Scientists estimate that 95,000 giraffes live in Africa today. Zoos try to breed giraffes to increase their population. The Department of African Parks, and African governments also help to protect giraffes. It is up to humans to prevent giraffes from disappearing.

Giraffe Facts

Scientific Name: Giraffa camelopardalis

Shoulder Height: 10-16 feet (3–4.9 m) at the shoulder

Weight: Males weigh up to 3,000 pounds (1,360.8 kg), females weigh up to 2,500 pounds (1,133 kg)

Color: dark brown with cream spots, variety of patterns depending upon subspecies

Reaches sexual maturity at: 4 years in females, 7 in males

Gestation (pregnancy period): 15 months

Litter Size: Usually one calf at a time

Favorite Food: Leaves, grasses, bark, roots, seedpods, fruit, especially acacia leaves

Range: A narrow area across Central Africa, and in a small section of South Africa.

Glossary

Bachelor Group An all-male group of giraffes

Cartilage This substance makes up joints, noses, and ears. Giraffe's horns have cartilage in them.

Cud A partially digested lump of food

Gestation Period The amount of time that a female is pregnant

Neck-knocking Fighting between giraffes to determine the leader of the group

Further Reading

Books

Arnold, Caroline. *Giraffe*. New York: William Morrow and Co., 1987.

Denis-Huot, Christine and Michel. *The Giraffe, a Living Tower*. Boston: Charlesbridge Publishing, 1993.

Sattler, Helen R. *Giraffes, Sentinels of the Savannas*. New York: Lothrop, Lee, and Shepard Books, 1990.

Sherr, Lynn. *Tall Blondes*. St. Louis: Andrews McMeel Publishing, 1997.

Web sites

Defenders of Wildlife Giraffe Page
http://www.kidsplanet.org/factsheets/giraffe.html

Oakland Zoo Giraffe Page
http://www.oaklandzoo.org/atoz/azgiraf.html

Giraffe Fun Fact Page
http://www.gustown.com/giraffe/rae12.HTML

Index